PERFACET

If you love the way you love,
then let me step back,
reroute stepping back into mine,
mine has more to come,
you got yours but I'm not peeping,
totally focused on the next season reapings,
as the fall predicts winters seasoned,
to resurrect springs down south,
of this part of the globe,
though knowing near the equator,
is the place where everything grows,
so eye respect your check,
in your game of life,
without playing it,
eye got many more moves,
without reality displaying them,
eye work hard when I'm at rest,
controlling my so called dreams,
building the next after next,
then eyes peel back remembering,
what was built to step into what was built . . . .

You said i couldn't
i got it touched
you know loves...

You said i couldn't
locked down waiting so long
another love is grown...

You said i couldn't
silly you without vue
loves i keep grabbing it...

You said i couldn't
then closed the door back
hands in the air eyes shut...

You said i couldn't
then walked to jump under the covers
peeking like we can't have it...

You said i couldn't
love turned the lights off
and you felt i could.

Introduction

Reaching the heights in my life,

I got inked into my skin,

not fore a show as some do,

but fore a symbolic meaning,

of feeling the pain leave the body,

indeed it is intense so much,

you want to drop a tear,

but me take all societal views against me,

begin needle across me skin,

release life's imperfections,

now look at me now,

art of perfection.

I'm like everything you thought up,
erased, reflipped, remixed,
in hopes of deletion,
but you forgot eye am inked in.

I'm like ah character with a limitless pen,
sentencing every reverb echoing playwright scenes,
flipping pages performing skits and loves heaven enriched,
with passionate fluid flowing ah lover's movement,
connecting nervous beginnings,
networking your every nervous ending,
systematically touching outer spacious spots,
soothing sipping smooth over my rock,
crushed and broken down into pieces of peace,
drinking ambition and endeavor up now,
fueling hearts with more rhythm and times,
beating concoctions as the sound off of this understanding,
of who I'm like while in your zone enhancing communication,
via telepathetic messaging written fore your eyes imagining bliss's
transcendence....

I'm like everything you thought up,
erased, reflipped, remixed,
in hopes of deletion,
but you forgot eye am inked in.

January 2014

Wind carried me,
dropped me into earth,
gaia knew perfection,
hardness became imperfect,
softness spouted,
i see shines perceptively,
blackbird of intelligence,
spoke to me,
all the way,
then released me,
into wind,
i know,
i took,
you everywhere,
and i feel the same,
too . . . .
Seas,
i can easily touch ground,
deepest,
a brush of shallow,

reflections,
under sun,
wavy moon lights,
which one am i,
of all personalities,
that are just aspects,
of everything?
I am still walking . . .
yet me been many places,
practiced many religions,
i found faith in myself,
there is no religion of self,
though my faith is strong,
i express of me best i can,
due to limits below,
of hue-man languages,
animals have tongues,
other kingdoms play signs,
act accordingly aware,
then again maybe blind.
Fire,
me too have no home,

we spark sudden,
ignite fury of flames,
a remembrance,
every arsonist tame,
pyromaniac in nature,
or neteru,
soon one burn simmer,
simmer ashes out,
providing fertile ground,
earth is deeper than expected,
accepting even death as life,
a birth of anew sight,
delightful memory,
cheers to you roots,
i grow altitude,
wherever planet-wise,
wild and uncut,
change of four,
cores of must,
detached from outer,
inner sown soul we tale,
seed of the unknown.

I find a home,

grow a little bit,

then home evicts me,

reasons are known,

me is bold,

they say go,

oh no you cannot,

i am not elegant,

neither are you,

the world thrills me,

she is fine with cute,

he is sugar to be dilute,

fill me up flavor now,

won my suggestion,

guzzled the digestion,

watched progression,

settled in no aggression,

yet trouble finds me,

no you cannot stay,

and like dog . . .

i roam all alone,

eyes forward,

while peripheral,

again another experience,

the path chosen,

within me seek,

to grow further,

as seed of the unknown.

How did you,
get into my bathroom?
On the brown papertowel roll,
though at first you fell,
from the lights,
above the sink mirror,
and later i found you . . .
must be my lucky day,
must be my lucky week,
must be my lucky month,
must be my lucky year,
you have ancestors too,
how great you are,
shift onto my soft finger,
colorblind you are,
now we going outside,
where the sun is shining bright,
though cold you warmed my inner,
oh you do not want to leave me,
well here . . . a little roll now,
let your legs feel the brick's edge,
in the sunlight shine brightly,
my ladybug.

Me arms stretch wide,
i stand rooted,
a silhouette,
waters within me hug,
imagine me arms,
elbows to forearms,
the branches to hands,
hands composed as keys,
ebony and ivory tips,
encircles calm sea,
standing as willow,
me formed the waters,
finally me did,
me knew it,
though when i fall,
leaves of autumn,
stroll along i say,
i say to me,
now the calm sea,
is yours again friend,
enjoy your position,
in life unmoved,
still though not able,
to hug it all,
you can meditate,
happiness smiling,
alone.

Moment on,
sea way,
sizzle around me,
hot touches,
curly curl curls curled,
inside each other smooch,
you were there,
what happened?
Your mistiness sets-in,
upon my full lips,
etched-in crevices,
deep ditches of dew,
sweetened of your grace,
wise you are,
mush gently,
push through tongue,
me want to taste,
tantalizing,
moist and splendid,
the feeling.

Flames,

turn and twist,

crackle and pop,

elevate nonstop,

the sight is fury,

within ablaze,

never stop,

keep cinders bottom,

one day and night,

trailing on arrival,

meet me chiller,

thaw out cautious,

step aside,

let me keep going,

stacking fires,

all out figured,

amplify.

In the air,
live and uncut,
naturally designed,
darkest flight,
cloak of gaseous embers,
i saw you creep,
and the owl know us deep,
thought of movement,
heated,
strapped,
safety approaches,
no water please,
blow in your breath,
increase me,
tale a story,
write a folk,
be a myth,
setup attention,
span emotions,
gathered common,
all inn,
do not touch,
slowly naked,
under protection,
cove happily,
sleep in luminosity.

Connector,

a nervous system,

lit up,

within,

glass of spectacular,

we stand humble,

you turn on and off,

manually,

built to last,

even,

when my eyelids drop,

me eyelashes curl up,

appealing feeling,

i am touched,

electrified too,

on-sight aspired,

two in-tuned,

brightening,

yet dark,

angling corners,

an expressionist,

texture who colors,

wattage of fusion,

silence and illusion,

duo under the influence,

of lampshade.

On me,
me and you,
in the snow,
my feet,
show my prints,
sitting on log,
below surviving temperature,
i am here dear,
my will is hearth,
spirited fiery,
churning,
three sixty,
per degree,
beating harder,
the hearts are calling,
stampede of realest,
searing perspiration,
bare and stark,
raw and unprotected,
stood up professing,
echoing known,
i am glow!

No you ain't,

i am tired,

the revival,

upcoming,

the rise,

swollen,

expansion,

too much,

unload,

oblivion,

aftershock,

spreads wide infinity,

held in awaiting,

way too long,

my combustion.

I felt you,

touch you too,

i know you too,

we flew like magpies,

in the mirror is true,

up higher,

dip flyer,

never dire,

coasting,

wings of fire,

tornado of inferno,

metaturned up fueled,

spray me out,

catch me clout,

stop listening,

feel the glistening,

up closest,

dramacydal,

everywhere,

play of black love,

full sail,

forest fire,

on land,

hurricane on land,

total encompassed,

nowhere to go,

rolling and controlling,

flipping isms,

intense in my rhythms,

i felt your soul.

On boulders,
by myself,
thinking,
breathing,
outlook,
a pebble,
in my right hand,
left out empty,
throw it no,
skip my destiny,
how far ripples,
perform,
they perform,
perform shows,
so dark below,
let me strip,
the world is sleep,
night same as my body,
darker than dark,
shine on me,
taking my plunge,
into the neverending,
reflecting my fate,
at night.

Into the depths,
without air,
released,
before,
elemental planes,
were broken,
falling,
failing,
feeling,
drowning,
softly,
intake,
ounces,
gallons,
drowning,
lungs fulfilled,
prophecy,
revealed,
arms out,
no more pain,
last smile,
and tears,
performed,
at night.

Why me?
Dayum . . .
and so i stare,
the glare is real,
still waving,
the waters,
riveting,
ill,
shellshocked,
memories repeating,
battling me,
they war at me,
shaking my head,
no!! no!!
Not now . . .
I get up,
quickly,
and the reflection,
my reflection,
jumps out,
from beyond,
and begs me,
to stay with him,
at night.

Like a gust of speed,

slow within,

the deception of how,

when is quickest,

why is the reasoning,

thin with thickness,

you turned on me,

sow at highest speed,

i will uplift you,

off your feet,

completely,

gone,

you in the past,

cause,

i am,

coming . . .

coming . . .

coming . . . .

Fore real,
life is appealing,
constants,
signs,
symbols,
numbers,
the flashes,
lights brighten,
the feeling,
it is realer,
who peeled out,
who mashed out,
who dashed out,
who walking,
who talking,
who holding,
who sold out,
who got in,
who broke up,
who done it,
at night.

Still tripping,

not caring,

throwing up,

sick as ill,

you like it,

don't fight it,

no wisdom,

steel busting,

she thought,

he said,

somebody,

resting in piss,

finally...

at night.

Stories,

mothers,

children,

you,

me,

nature,

air,

the air,

the air breathe,

the air breathe still,

the air breathe still needing,

the air breathe still needing none,

and water,

water bubbles,

water evaporates,

water sizzles,

water temper,

you coming at me,

your talk is wrong on me,

you coming at me foul,

outer park home run now!

My Queens,
the three,
tattooed on me,
militant body,
represent,
our justice,
our fierceness,
our depths,
they say,
sun never dull,
true hearts moon,
in the loves,
against war,
never shed,
one tear,
your heart,
best not,
beat no fear,
my three Queens,
don't shed,
no tears,
so our hearts,
beat no fear,
our hearts,
shed no tears.

Stand up,
bravest,
what you about,
i breathe left,
Nefertiti,
i breathe right,
Nzinga,
from me bellow,
is Tubman,
we ain't dead,
straight live,
the power,
amplified,
our skin,
is moving,
the fire,
volcano,
eruption,
lava flows,
together,
we blast,
zero,

one,
two,
three,
four,
five,
six,
seven,
eight,
nine,
come again,
all into you,
as the host,
with our most,
oppression,
we smite,
depression,
we smite,
destroy,
at all cost,
dusted,
on the mash,
railing,

with no brakes,
gulfstream of fate,
hurricane of flames,
electrified twisters,
out the skies,
outer mind,
outer body,
morning star,
evening star,
walking one,
of tremendous,
relentless emotion,
soulfully spirited,
on arrival,
adversary no escape,
quake of difference,
chasm calling captured foes,
falling surrounded by bye bye,
all in endless,
echoing neverending,
grasping they gone,
sentenced crushed boomed!

www.ingramcontent.com/pod-product-compliance
Lightning Source LLC
Chambersburg PA
CBHW070730180526
45167CB00004B/1691